MW01284294

For The Love of Scarves: Infinity and Beyond!

8 Knitting Patterns for Beginners

Tammy Asselin

ABOUT THE AUTHOR

Tammy Asselin grew up in a French Canadian family in Northern Ontario, Canada where knitting, crafting, sewing and home cooking were part of her heritage. Her first childhood memories include images of her mother with hands that were always busy creating. One room of the house was designated as the "sewing room", where all of the treasures used to create could be found. Generations of women in her family gathered in the kitchens of their homes where they worked on individual and group projects, all the while chatting and enjoying one another's company. The children were always welcome to join and it was no wonder that Tammy found herself with a curiosity and a desire to join these women in their camaraderie, resulting in beautiful hand crafted works of art. Whatever the trend of the time; macramé, liquid or Japanese embroidery, sewing, latch hooking, cross stitching, ceramics, papier maché, crocheting or knitting, the results were spectacular! It was however, the love of knitting that remained the constant for her throughout the years.

Although many of those women who first inspired her have since passed away, the tradition of "crafting", and reminiscing of days gone by, lives on in her home.

The Northern Ontario community where she grew up continues to be her home. Tammy married a "home town boy" and enjoys the simple, quiet life with her husband and two sons.

OTHER BOOKS BY THE AUTHOR

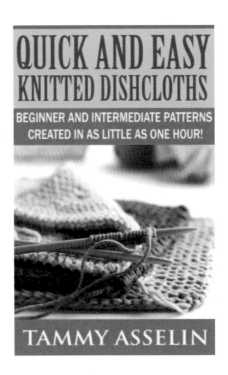

ACKNOWLEDGEMENTS

I would like to extend a very special thank you to each of the models for this book! Each of them indulged me for a photo session in the outdoors, on days when temperatures were very cold! I have known each the younger models since they were little girls and have enjoyed watching them become young women; each as beautiful on the inside as on the outside! The more "mature" models have been my long-time friends, going back to when we were teenagers some thirty five years ago. My sincere thanks and appreciation to each of you:

- Amélie Samson
- Callie Paddock
- Connie Gerrior
- Kendi Morden
- Renee Baronette

Additional thanks are also extended to my sister-in-law Barb Asselin, for the inspiration and the guidance to put my ideas and creations on paper and get them published!

Lastly, to my family: Paul, Jarett and Noah, for their love, and ongoing support and encouragement for all of my projects and interests.

WHY YOU SHOULD READ THIS BOOK

Have you had an interest in learning to knit, but didn't know where to get started?

Have you been intimidated by the complicated patterns of difficult projects?

Would you like to get started with a small project that can be completed in a short period of time?

Have you admired the new trend of cowl and infinity scarves?

Would you like to wear a unique handcrafted creation made by you?

Do you like to give unique handcrafted gifts?

Are you looking for a pattern to teach to a younger knitter in your life?

If you answered "yes" to any of these questions, this book is for you!

In this book, you will find:

- a review of the main knitting stitches and materials used for scarves, for new knitters

- a description of the abbreviations for knitting stitches commonly used

- 8 patterns for completed scarves; straight, cowl and infinity, using only knit and purl stitches

- PLUS accompanying photo images of each scarf to allow you to see the finished results.

Are you ready to get started? Browse through the patterns, pick a favorite, choose your yarn, get your knitting needles and you are ready to begin!

FOR THE LOVE OF SCARVES: INFINITY AND BEYOND!

8 KNITTING PATTERNS FOR BEGINNERS

TABLE OF CONTENTS

INTRODUCTION

Thank you for purchasing this book of my favorite scarf patterns for the beginner knitter. My first knitting project was a scarf when I was 12 years old. I can still recall the uneven tension and the dropped stitches, but regardless of its' imperfections, I wore that scarf with pride! After completing my first scarf, I did not return to knitting until I was approximately 18 years old. I was hundreds of miles from home and with my "beginner booklet"; I followed the diagrams and had many long distance conversations with my mother, while she tried to explain how to cast on and off, and how to decrease and increase stitches, over the telephone. This was long before the days of the Internet and videos where one can learn to knit while following along on a video.

When I graduated from post-secondary education and returned home for my first "real" job, I spent many long winter nights learning to knit much more complicated patterns from my mother and her friends. For several years, I proudly wore many sweaters of intricate patterns hand knit by me. In addition, I enjoyed completing several unique creations for nieces, nephews, new babies and friends. Following the birth of my own sons, there was a gap of several years when I did not have time to complete any intricate patterns and stuck to the simpler knitting projects, such as scarves. With so many available options of yarn, I was hooked and began experimenting with yarn, needle sizes and patterns.

Over the past several years, knitted scarves, especially cowls and infinity loops have become the trend.

There are many terms used to describe these scarves, such as cowls, infinity and snood, however, for this book, I will refer to cowls and infinity scarves. The definition used by me for a cowl, is a circular scarf, which is shorter than the infinity scarf, it cannot be doubled and it resembles a tube. The definition for the infinity scarf is one that can be worn in a single loop and is much longer, or it can be looped once, twice or three times around the neck. Cowl and infinity scarves can be knitted using two straight needles and sewn together or knit on a circular needle, requiring no sewing. Scarves which are knit on straight needles can also remain straight rather than sewn together to create a loop.

In this book, I have chosen to provide eight of the easiest level patterns for beginners, with a gradual introduction to a change in stitch patterns. New knitters can start with the garter stitch, which is a repeat of knit rows. Stocking stitch is introduced in the second pattern where a combination of garter and stocking stitch patterns are combined. Next, the knit and purl stitches are alternated creating the seed or moss stitch on straight needles, as well as a circular needle, providing completely different results due to the type of yarn and needle size. Additional patterns are variations of these stitches with different yarn and needle sizes.

Please note that this book is not an instructional book to learn to knit, but does provide patterns, as well as descriptive explanations of stitches for those already familiar with the basics of knitting. An individual who has never picked up a set of knitting needles may find it helpful to consult "how to" or "learn to knit" books, in addition to videos which provide visual demonstrations and instructions.

I do not promote one brand of yarn over another however I did provide the details as to the brand and type of yarn used for each pattern to offer a variety of alternatives when choosing yarn. The measurements provided for the completed scarves are an approximation of what you can expect, but will be determined by your knitting tension. My knitting is neither tight nor loose, but can be considered standard or regular tension.

The time required to complete a scarf will vary according to the pattern, size of yarn and needles and the skill level of the knitter. The simplest beginner pattern, with larger needles and an experienced knitter can be accomplished in as little as an evening whereas a beginner may require a little more time. I have found that I can generally complete a scarf with ease over a weekend or two or three evenings.

If you are ready, it's time to get started! I hope you enjoy the variety of beginner patterns for scarves, as well as develop a passion for the craft and get hooked on knitting!

YARN

There are a wide variety of yarns to choose from, depending on the look of the project you are making. You can choose from very fine yarn which offers the best results with smaller size knitting needles to the mega bulky yarn which is knit with very large needles. The larger the yarn and the needles, the quicker the project is completed. It's easy to be overwhelmed by all the choices available; how do you know which yarn is right for your project? Many new knitters prefer to use the exact type of yarn suggested in the pattern, but that is not necessary.

There are many combinations of cotton, acrylic, polyester, ribbon, nylon, wool, alpaca, hemp, rayon, cashmere, mohair, silk, linen, bouclé and chenille. Yarn can also be found with a metallic look, with sequins or payettes. The options are endless! All knitting yarn is made from either natural or synthetic fibers. When choosing the yarn for your project, take into consideration the look you want to achieve, the weight of the yarn, as well as washing instructions, as not all yarns are created equal!

First time knitters may prefer a variegated colour which is much more forgiving as mistakes are less noticeable. For a more intricate pattern, you may choose a solid colour to allow the pattern to be more visible. Yarns can also be combined by knitting with two different colours or types of yarn creating a unique look. Explore the options available and have some fun!

KNITTING NEEDLE CONVERSION CHART

METRIC	U.S.	U.K.
2mm	0	14
2.25mm	1	13
2.75mm	2	12
3mm	-	11
3.25mm	3	10
3.5mm	4	-
3.75mm	5	9
4mm	6	8
4.5mm	7	7
5mm	8	6
5.5mm	9	5
6mm	10	4
6.5mm	10½	3
7mm	-	2
7.5mm	-	1
8mm	11	0
9mm	13	00
10mm	15	000
12mm	17	-
16mm	19	-
19mm	35	-
25mm	50	-

ABBREVIATIONS AND INSTRUCTIONS

ABBREVIATIONS

KNITTING TERMINOLOGY

Knit – K

Purl – P

Stitches – st(s)

Bind off – Cast off

INSTRUCTIONS

(*) – work instructions following the * as many more times as indicated in the first instruction

Tension/Gauge – this refers to the finished tension or gauge of the knitted work. Tension will be determined by the size of knitting needles, yarn, as well as knitting experience. Maintaining a consistent tension will develop with time.

Garter Stitch – a repeat of knit rows

Stocking Stitch – a combination of alternating a knit row, followed by a purl row

Seed Stitch/Moss Stitch – alternating a knit stitch and a purl stitch

1. BASIC GARTER STITCH SCARF

Materials:

2 balls of *Loops & Threads "1st Kiss"* Bulky yarn (100g/3.5oz; 100m/110yds)

Size 12.75 mm/ US 17 Knitting Needles

Measurements:

30cm width x 80cm length (11.5" x 31") 62" circumference

Instructions:

Cast on 22 stitches.

Knit across all stitches on all rows.

Knit to desired length.

Cast off.

Weave in ends.

Block with a damp cloth.

This scarf can remain straight or can be sewn together for the resulting infinity loop scarf.

*Note: This is an ideal first pattern for the first time knitter. Practicing this repeat of knit stitches will allow the beginner knitter to develop a consistency with tension and familiarity with the knit stitch.

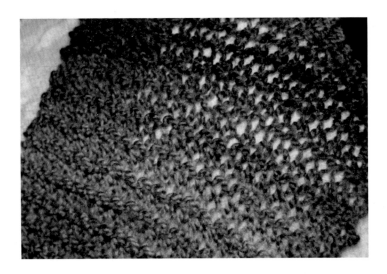

2. BEGINNER STRIPED SCARF (VERSION 1)

Materials:

2 balls *Loops & Threads "Opus"* Super Bulky yarn (100g/3.5oz; 38 m/42 yds)

Size 12.75 mm/US 17 Knitting Needles

Measurements:

25cm width x 82cm length (9.5" x 32") 64" circumference

Instructions:

(As seen on the model on the left, in the blue/red/orange multicolor scarf).

Cast on 16 stitches.

Rows 1 – 5: Knit all rows (garter stitch).

Row 6:   Purl across.

Knit 10 rows stocking stitch (alternating knit and purl rows).

Knit 4 rows garter stitch (knit all rows).

Continue in this pattern until desired length, finishing with 4 knit rows.

Cast off.

Weave in ends.

This scarf can remain straight or can be sewn together for the resulting infinity loop scarf.

Block with a damp cloth.

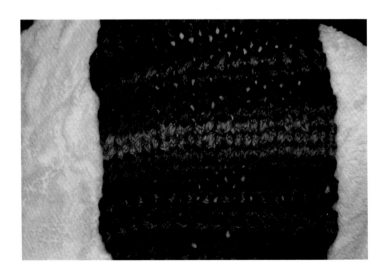

3. BEGINNER STRIPED SCARF (VERSION 2)

Materials:

2 balls *Loops & Threads "Opus"* Super Bulky yarn (100g/3.5oz; 38 m/42yds)

Size 12.75 mm/US 17 Knitting Needles

Measurements:

22cm width x 68cm length (8.5" x 26.5") 53" circumference

Instructions:

Cast on 16 stitches.

Rows 1 – 5: Knit across (garter stitch rows).

Row 6: Knit 2, Purl across to last 2 stitches on row, Knit 2.

Knit in stocking stitch for 4 rows (alternating one knit and one purl row, always knitting first and last 2 stitches on each purl row).

Knit 10 rows (garter stitch).

Continue in this pattern to desired length, ending with 4 knit rows.

Cast off.

Weave in ends.

This scarf can remain straight or can be sewn together for the resulting infinity loop scarf.

Block with a damp cloth.

*Note: Knitting 2 stitches at the beginning and end of each purl row will prevent the scarf from rolling inwards.

**Note: These two variations are also ideal patterns for the new knitter with the introduction of the purl stitch, as well as the bulky yarn and large needles which allows the knitter to see the stitches more easily. It is a quick project to complete giving the knitter a sense of accomplishment! The two patterns are very similar in that they are a reversal of the number of garter and stocking stitch rows. Feel free to make any adjustment to the number of rows or stitches for this pattern.

4. SEED STITCH INFINITY SCARF (VERSION 1)

Materials:

2 balls Bernat *"Roving"* Bulky yarn (100g/3.5oz; 109 m/120yds)

Size 6.5 mm/US 10.5 Circular Knitting Needle (65-80cm – 29"-36")

Stitch marker

Measurements:

22cm width x 90cm length (8.5" x 35") 70" circumference

Instructions:

Cast on 139 stitches.

Place a stitch marker at the beginning of round on the right hand needle and join by working the first stitch on the left needle to the right needle, being careful not to twist the stitches.

Knit 1, Purl 1 in round.

Continue in pattern until desired length.

Cast off in pattern.

Weave in ends.

Block with a damp cloth.

5. SEED STITCH SCARF (VERSION 2)

Materials:

2 balls *Bernat "Mega Bulky"* yarn (200g/7oz; 38m/42yds)

Size 19 mm/US 35 Knitting Needles

Measurements:

26cm width x 74cm length (10" x 29") 58" circumference

Instructions:

Cast on 10 stitches.

Row 1: Knit 1, Purl 1, repeat to end of row.

Row 2: Purl 1, Knit 1, repeat to end of row.

Repeat these 2 rows for seed stitch pattern until desired length, ending with a row 1.

Cast off in pattern.

Weave in ends.

This scarf can remain straight or can be sewn together for the resulting infinity loop scarf.

Block with a damp cloth.

*Note: This scarf can be knit in an evening due to the super bulky weight and the large knitting needles.

**Note: Although this scarf follows the same seed stitch pattern as the previous *#4 Seed Stitch Infinity Scarf,* the different weight of yarn and size of the knitting needles provides a very different end result.

6. RIBBED SCARF

Materials:

1 ball of *Red Heart "Super Saver"* Chunky (141gr/5oz; 215m/236yds)

Size 6 mm/US 10 Knitting Needles

Measurements:

20cm width x 83cm length (7.75" x 32.5") 65" circumference

Instructions:

Cast on 35 stitches.

Row 1: Knit 3, Purl 2, repeat to end of row.

Row 2: Purl 1, Knit 1.

Repeat these 2 rows for pattern and continue until desired length.

Cast off in pattern.

Weave in ends.

Scarf can remain straight or can be sewn together to form the infinity loop.

Block with a damp cloth.

7. RIBBED INFINITY SCARF

Materials:

2 balls *Red Heart "Light & Lofty"* Super Bulky (170g/6oz; 128m/140yds)

Size 9 mm/US 15 Circular Knitting Needle (65-80cm – 29-36")

Stitch marker

Measurements:

30cm width x 74cm length (11.5"x 29") 58" circumference

Instructions:

Cast on 100 stitches.

Place stitch marker at beginning of round on right hand needle and join by working the first stitch on left hand needle to the right hand needle being careful not to twist the stitches.

Row 1: * Knit 2, Purl 2; repeat to end of round.

Row 2: Knit 1,* Purl 2, Knit 2; repeat from * to last 3 stitches, Purl 2, Knit 1.

Repeat these 2 rows in round until desired length, approximately 45 cm (18 inches) from beginning.

Cast off in pattern.

Weave in ends.

Block with a damp cloth.

8. SPIRAL INFINITY SCARF

Materials:

2+ balls *Patons "Colorwul"* Bulky (85g/3oz; 81m/91yds)

Size 9mm/US 13 Circular Knitting Needle (70-91 cm/32-36")

Stitch marker

Measurements:

28.5cm width x 56.5cm length (11" x 22") 44" circumference

Instructions:

Cast on 104 stitches (or any multiple of a repeat of 3, minus 1).

Place stitch marker at beginning of round on right hand needle and join by working the first stitch on left hand needle to the right hand needle being careful not to twist the stitches.

Row 1: Knit 2, Purl 1; repeat to end of round.

Repeat this row and continue in pattern. The purl stitch will move over one stitch in each round creating the spiral.

Continue in pattern until desired length, approximately 11" wide.

Cast off loosely.

Weave in ends.

Block with a damp cloth.

Note: If you prefer a looser fit cowl when doubled, I would recommend casting on 155 stitches.

CONCLUSION

Hopefully, you enjoyed this beginner knitting pattern book for straight, cowl and infinity scarves! If you are a new knitter or still consider yourself a beginner, you may feel most confident knitting several of these patterns before moving on to more intricate patterns. Perhaps this was your first experience knitting with circular needles, which can take some getting used to, but become a preferred tool for many knitters. You may have also experimented with a variety of yarn and knitting needle sizes and have developed a personal preference for knitting with fine, medium or chunky weight yarn, as well as a favorite size of knitting needles. The possibilities are endless with a simple change of yarn and needle sizes!

The intention of this book was to provide new and non-knitters with some first projects to undertake that were fairly simple and easily accomplished in a short period of time. If you are interested, a second book is also available for knitters with more experience. If you are feeling confident and comfortable with the basic knit and purl stitches, perhaps you are ready to take on an intermediate pattern. Please check my other book *"For the Love of Scarves: Infinity and Beyond! 9 Intermediate Knitting Patterns"*.

Wear your new scarf or scarves with pride! Or maybe you have chosen to share your new talent with friends and family and have gifted others? I hope you are getting compliments on your new fashion accessory! For the love of scarves and for the love of knitting, have some fun, take some risks and continue to experiment with stitches and patterns!

REVIEWS

I hope that you enjoyed this book and that the knitting instructions were clear, that the photos were helpful and that you were successful at completing your first or several hand knitted scarves.

As a self-published author, this is my second knitting book and it would be greatly appreciated, if you would be willing to provide me with some feedback. I plan to continue to share some of my creations for different projects, so if you are willing, please leave a review for me at the Amazon page for this book. Your support is greatly appreciated!

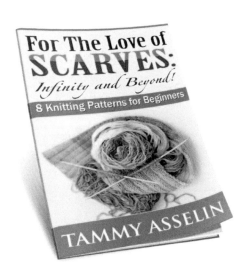

Made in the USA
Middletown, DE
08 October 2018